I Don't March to the Beat of a Different Drummer: I'm the Whole Band

I Don't March to the Beat of a Different Drummer: I'm the Whole Band

✦

Perceptions of a Bipoloar Life

By Leslie Jay

iUniverse, Inc.
New York Lincoln Shanghai

I Don't March to the Beat of a Different Drummer: I'm the Whole Band

Perceptions of a Bipoloar Life

All Rights Reserved © 2004 by Jim Lytton

No part of this book may be reproduced or transmitted in any form or by any means, graphic, electronic, or mechanical, including photocopying, recording, taping, or by any information storage retrieval system, without the written permission of the publisher.

iUniverse, Inc.

For information address:
iUniverse, Inc.
2021 Pine Lake Road, Suite 100
Lincoln, NE 68512
www.iuniverse.com

ISBN: 0-595-30649-7

Printed in the United States of America

For Alan.

Contents

Acknowledgements

Some of the People that made this tome possible, God bless em':

My brother Jim and his family
My cousin Don who gave me more than I could hazard to ask
Doctor David Altman
Doctor Severance Kelley
Doctor Marcel Neumann
Doctor Robert Bradley
Doctor K. Rangel
Doctor M. Carey
Doctor E. Alvarez
Doctor C. Zeller
Doctor E. Johnson
Doctor Rennick
Doctor Pearson
Doctor Steve Pierce
Dr. T. Vaca-Haase
Mary McAffee RN, MS
Melinda Williams
Dan and Lupe' Scholl
Fran and John James
And to all of the others who know that <u>I know</u>.

To My Editor

A thousand thanks, to Bill James, who gave me the strength to write this book. Mr. James, an author in his own right, took time from his busy schedule to shepherd these ideas. He and my Guardian Angel have my heartfelt thanks.

Bias: "A particular tendency or inclination especially one that prevents unprejudiced consideration of a question; prejudice".

You do not look sick.
You do not act like you are nuts.
You do not have anything wrong with you.

The answer, the bias is simple.

<u>If you're not cut and bleeding</u>,
<u>You're not ill!</u>

Read on—

Welcome

Many of us are looking for a way to understand the lost dollars, jobs, years and families that result from the varied manifestations of the bipolar disorder.

These distressing times are peppered with other issues, from internal or external pressures of life, as we live it, to genetic and hormonal factors.

How can we put these issues that seem to keep us at our worst, to rest?

A simple formula exists: Give it shape, volume and form, and it will be understood.

A famous quotation speaks to this issue: "We have nothing to fear but fear itself."

Work with me on this one: imagine yourself standing on the middle line of a straight road that reaches far into the horizon. As you look down that road it seems that the shape is a very thin triangle that is wide where you are standing yet comes to an apex seemingly joining together in the far distance. Got it? Good.

Now look at the mix: Our pain, delusions, debts, anger, depression, the whole cornucopia of ills that we feel, is on one side of that disappearing highway, and life as it is, on the other.

Both sides join together at the hip so to speak. They are blended together to become the sum quality and quantity of the life that we lead.

We are faced with the decision to take the right first step, or to live in denial of the fact that the ills can be salved, that life can again happen fully, or even imperfectly, but always a whole lot better than the plate that we have been given in the first place.

We need the company of people who understand us because they go through the same concerns as we do. Support groups are very important, I'll tell you, the meetings, the clinic visits, the doctors' help, counseling, and the medicines give our lives substance and healing so they can flower to the max.

This little book is intended for you. Custom made. I have lived it and survived, and those that led to that healing are saluted.

Lets read on, and by the way, have a pen, pad and paper ready as well as the yellow pages of your town, and if you have Internet access, fire up that computer right now.

This book is an easy read, but it answers some concerns, opens doors, and who knows, you might even pass some of the information on to those you meet that are just starting to look for the answers. LJ

My Story

I lived in a small town in Florida, one of those places where the sidewalks rolled up by 5 pm, the front doors were never locked, and you knew everyone on your block.

My father was a professional man, his two brothers and himself in medicine as well as two sisters married to fine men. My mother a professional homemaker with three sisters and one brother, all blessed with talents in art, music, woodworking to name a few.

We lived in a small house until a few years later, when the "Dream Home" was built.

My parents started together and ended in divorce. My father had a bad temper, but at the same time loved me. He was an open fellow, however my mother preferred to be a private person, loving me as well. Hours of arguments signaled the end of their relationship. Many verbal battles were the order of the day, and many times I hid behind doorways and listened to their angry words, believing that their disagreements were entirely my fault. My fathers' temper was directed at me in ways that I could not understand at the time but came to accept. I know far better today. The instant, total anger was a signal that my father was bipolar, one more of his brothers was as well.

I am bipolar, my brother is not, however one of his two sons is bipolar. The facts are irrefutable, genes are genes and the magic ladder, DNA, determines when familial traits are more than just similar looks. My dad could not hold back his instant anger and moodiness. My mother was equal to the task. Mom got the house, and went to work, caring for my brother and I, and dad still had his practice and another home.

My father remarried years later; my mother remained divorced through the remainder of her life.

I loved my parents, but that type of love changed later, in a way that I never could have dreamed of. Both have passed away, but I maintain a good relationship with my stepmother.

My years as a child were dismal. I was a sickly kid, and spent more time indoors looking out at a child's world than taking part in it. I always wondered why the kids beyond the screen door were playing outside and I could not.

I was argumentative, and had destructive anger spells that came up in an instant just like dads', and I suffered the exhaustion that followed. I always wanted what I wanted right then.

This is a warning sign to be aware of.

I napped in a couch on the sun porch, which had a tile roof. I had an invisible friend that talked to me.

I was most calm during rainstorms listening to the drops pitter- patter above me. Much later in life I was given a sound generator, it played the sound of waves, the bubbling brook and tropical rainstorms. I found the rainstorm and the bubbling brook to be very calming.

I later gave it to my nephew who found it to be comforting. That's right, the rainstorm and the bubbling brook seems to help the bipolar to stay calm.

I had a problem with losing things, not remembering where I had put them, and blaming everyone including the deity for taking my "stuff" and feeling embarrassed when my parents or my own discovery of the item proved me wrong. Anger would ensue. Later in life I found that the addition of psychotic features and schizoid effective conditions caused me to hear voices and loose things, even claim that they were stolen. Medicines today help these conditions.

I had few real friends, and that seemed to be a format for the rest of my young life.

I did not know what I was missing. Looking back, the common practice of taking a nap with falling rain and gray skies seemed to make things better, but later in life dark snowy days an no sunshine made me dull and unhappy. That was a warning sign that I later came to know as depression, but a clue to fight what is called the *seasonal effect.*

I was introduced to my baby brother, seven and a half years younger than myself, a tiny fellow asleep in a blanket on my mothers lap, seated in the back of the family car, while we were heading home from the hospital and my first thoughts were how he would fit into my portion of the pie of love and attention.

I was a poor student, and I was more of a class problem than I knew. I went through kindergarten, first grade, and then second. Third grade was the turning point for me—I was held back to take the classes again and that year changed my life forever. I gave up.

Psychotherapy helped me greatly, many years later. My parents could not understand my anger spates, or excess sleeping, as well as bad grades and illegible handwriting, so they decided to take me to the "big city" to visit a child psychiatrist and a psychologist. To this day I remember the name of the psychiatrist, he was one of the finest people that I ever met in this life. The psychologist was the opposite. (There are good people and bad in all professions, keep an open mind as you choose, be comfortable with your health professional.) The psychiatrist did not prescribe any medications, but the session went well. The tests the psychologist gave were a nightmare. Something the guy said burned itself into my mind and it remains there today. He said, "You are an angry child and cannot love." I was shocked and I felt that I had been betrayed. I went home to the kind intentions of my parents, who both said, "You should be better now." A few years later I visited a psychiatrist in town for sessions but nothing seemed to change with the anger and the depression. School however, seemed better.

A few years of mediocre performance in elementary school gave me little joy but the grades passed me to junior high and the depression seemed to subside a bit. Anger however seemed to be my downfall. I enjoyed the weather, the beach, and cementing relationships with three friends who to this day are held sacred to my heart. I was still plagued by illnesses that kept me sidelined from an ordinary life. My brother and I learned a lot from each other even though we took turns living at the other parents' houses, and playing on the feelings of each of our folks. Both of us learned to enjoy music, a legacy from my mother and her side of the family. My brother developed a penchant for music, as did I. Make no mistake; there were good times as well. The sunny days left me enervated and better, the dark cloudy days left me disconsolate and tired. I have learned that sunlight is needed for some of us to feel better. Natural sunlight can be duplicated for those of us with seasonal effect to make us feel much better. Cloudy or dark snowy or rainy days seem to sap my strength. The answer for those of us with seasonal concerns is to make use of light bars or bulbs that are designed to provide the same conditions as daylight. I put several bulbs marked "daylight" in the bathroom light fixture in my apartment and I spent every morning in enervating light before going to work. Lighting at work can be fitted with this kind of illumination as well.

By the time that I was in junior high, the sole job seemed to be playing in band and the other lessons be damned. I began reading and soon it became a major preoccupation.

New worlds began to open; yet the reading was always done in bed, promoting bad vision, and causing me to sleep more.

I went through the norms—dating, a small car, small accidents in the car, and a surly attitude towards authority in school, but I was introduced to all of the wonders of the public library.

Music, however, was a great way to cover your problems and I took up clarinet lessons from the bandmaster of the city band. In a cold dank room I learned to play with some talent, but I exacerbated my mothers' frustration by not practicing.

I made it through junior high school and into senior high; I still had problems with excess sleep, but not knowing why. I do now. High school was a fine experience, but music was my forte'. The bandmaster was a great influence to me, and taught me a lot about music appreciation. The band even played at the Worlds Fair, giving me my first look at New York City. Some times the anger would flare at home as well in life, I had to be right, every one else was wrong and sleep seemed to be the answer. I felt that the bed was a kind of safe place. Not so! When I graduated from high school and a relative suggested that I join the Army, I did.

A note here—when we are in a manic state we cannot remember patches of time, facts, and we do not keep track of spending, that is where the spending problem of Grandiosity causes us to ask where did the money go?

Our attitudes seem to reign supreme and we know we are right except when we beat ourselves up for disastrous circumstances that occur unbidden to our eyes.

We also are wide open to other people's ideas; taking them as our own even if it breaks the law.

I went through basic training and studied at the Military School of Music.

All I could do was to try to practice, and get through the school. Weekends were dull and depression set in. I could hardly get out of bed. I went to my next duty station and played in the post band. Again, I could hardly get out of bed on weekends. A year later I was transferred to Germany, and I traveled to several countries during that year. But most days that passed I was busy. It seemed that as long as I was functioning at the job and the weather was sunny, depression and anger were non-existent. It was the best year of my life. (I should have stayed in the service!)

I later found out that I had thyroid problems that exacerbated the sluggishness and malaise. My focus upon leaving the service was to attend the junior college in town and transfer to a state college later. I was feeling good for a while, for weeks or months and then the defeatist attitude as well as excess sleep made short work of the time there and school ended.

Life went on. I played in a nightclub band for a while and worked construction.

I was given a job in a drug store and became assistant manager in a short amount of time, but I started obsessing over the job, working one or two days twenty-four hours at a time without rest at a fever pitch. Then the down side would occur, and I had to sleep one, two, or even three days to feel well. I was continually late for work even on a regular day, sleeping as if there was no tomorrow.

I had a couple of small businesses, and I began to realize that I could work some days and others would be a chore to get through. No actual thoughts about the past went through my mind and I had no idea that anything was wrong.

I went to Chicago to work with a family firm. I was given increasing responsibilities and my primary care physician in town suggested that due to my many visits to him for various ills, I should see a psychiatrist for some of them.

I was given several medicines and continued visits to both. My doctor mentioned that I had more ills than he expected to see in a man my age. I thought nothing of it at the time.

In 1994, I was diagnosed with type-2 diabetes and the pieces of the puzzle of my life began to fall into place. Bipolar people with diabetes may have up to 50% more real illnesses and diabetic neuropathies than the norm. My psychiatrist moved out of the state and I was referred to another good doctor. That's right, doctor. Never ever forget that your visit to a psychiatrist is to visit a medical doctor who spent a lot of years specializing in the help that we need.

The realities of life give us many gifts, one of which is the psychologist. Many of the discussions with the teamwork of psychiatrist and psychologist are the healing salve that is the answer to our needs. Choose your health professional with care. A couple once told me that they wanted the same comfort level as their most personal doctors when they both went for counseling. For you type "A" personalities out there: choose your mental health professional as you would your attorney and stockbroker.

The new doctor and my family doctor gave me several medicines that I took on a regular basis.

I got into major financial difficulties and lost ten years of profit sharing due to runaway credit card debt, lines of credit, as well as stock purchases totaling $120,000.00.

I purchased 600 books, 1,000 compact disks and loads of electronics and speakers.

I taped hundreds of TV shows on four video recorders and never took the time to watch them. Payments were made to pay off the debts, but more credit cards arrived and my debts soared.

I lost my will to do any thing but work, eat, sleep and buy things just as before. I never availed myself of the city of Chicago, the concerts, the plays, the art, and the sights to any great extent. I spent every penny that I earned for rent, food, auto insurance and repair and anything that struck my fancy. However, a wild card was in play. I had not been diagnosed as bipolar and I was given the wrong medicines not by intent or accident. They made it worse. Manic-depressive research and the bipolar state had few medicines for use at the time and treatment was in it's infancy, and not to the fore as well.

I lived to the rallying cry of the afflicted, "I want it and I want it now!"

I had no idea that there was a non-profit group similar to Alcoholics Anonymous, called Debtors Anonymous. These meetings help to salve the issues of indebtedness called Grandiosity (over spending), and the pressures of payments and the budget.

My profit sharing loss would have been less, had I known better.

I traveled the country and Canada for my employer, and got into bind after bind without knowing that I was digging my own grave. Work became an obsession, and my rushing to and fro, and then dropping into a sleep of the dead at night, left me without rest.

I had no idea that work stress was a problem until my psychiatrist told me that I should leave my job and go to work in a library. Unfortunately, I did not follow his advice.

My primary care doctor suggested seeing a specialist to set up a sleep test for sleep problems, restless legs, sleep apnea, and loss of good restive sleep. I did so and part of the problem was solved. I was given a c-pap breathing machine, which is portable and allows you a good REM sleep for a full night of rest. I still use one. It stops the snoring and sleep apnea, a condition where you can loose your breathing rhythm or even stop breathing for a while, interrupting the sleep cycle. By the way, if snoring is a problem, there is an answer, once, a lady told me that she slept in the bathroom because of the volume of her husbands' snoring, and was looking seriously at ending their relationship because of it. I told her about a device that I was using that solves the problem. I found a product called a "Clencher Quencher" while on a check up at my local dentist's office. A simple imprinting of your teeth takes place, and a form-fitted transparent plastic device that moves your lower jaw a slight bit forward is cast, preventing snoring. This device also stops Bruxing, the involuntary grinding of your teeth during sleep. Contact your family dentist for more information.

I worked out of Chicago for 14 years and had more and more trouble occurring month by month. I dreamed of having a home and a family, but instead I stayed in the same apartment all of the time in Chicago. I did not have time, (so I thought) to have a good private and social life. I was a workaholic. (Another aspect of depression.)

I started to get angry every time the mail that I had stacked up on the front table in my apartment tipped over, so I put it in a box. Magazines, private papers, work papers, everything went into boxes and at no time was I ever able to sort through it all. This happened so often that my apartment became filled with boxes almost to the ceilings. I had to restack boxes to move through the apartment. I could not get to my bed without moving boxes. I could not cook, (one of my loves) because the kitchen was full of boxes. Going to the bathroom was an adventure. I bought carryout food each night and ate it in bed, and then fell in to a deep sleep, or worked all night on paperwork that should take a half an hour to finish. The dust problem was horrid and the laundry next door got lots of business from me.

No one at work knew about my problem. I would put on my game face and would be dressed well each day for work. I kept a large suitcase at my workstation filled with paper work that I could not get around to. Drawers in my desk were filled with paperwork and "stuff," like good wine, aged over time and stored, destined never to see the light of day.

My desk was covered with stacks of paper that I called "my system". When I was on the road, I carried four large Samsonite Oyster suitcases. One was filled with clothes, another with books and magazines, one filled with paperwork, and the last with a portable compact disk player, speakers, compact disks, laptop computer, and a portable printer along with the obligatory multi plug surge protector and an extension cord. Needless to say, only the suitcase with the clothes would be opened.

The suitcases weighed 50 pounds each, and due to the weight and quantity required, many extra dollars were paid to taxis and airlines.

I was on a business trip to Toronto Canada, and had just cleared customs to return home to Chicago. I was dragging two luggage carts filled with two of the suitcases on each one, plus a clothing bag and the cases containing my c-pap machine, and a briefcase. I was overloaded to the max. I noticed a line of people that I had to break through to get to the waiting room for my flight. They were moving to a different flight area. Visualize this; it was the Chicago Bulls basketball team. I saw the tallest people that I had ever seen all together at one time, Mr. Jordan walked by, and I watched as several more of the team members walked in front of me. I decided that I should close my open mouth and try to establish what decorum I had left. At that moment Mr. Pippin looked at my load and me like I was from another planet, at that moment I became aware that there was something wrong with me. My thanks to Mr. Pippin for the awakening.

Here are a couple more of my experiences. I always knew how to do the right thing, my way. I was at a counter demonstration of my firms' products at a supply house, the day was finished and we were packing up to leave. A baby sparrow fell out of the eaves above us and landed with a thump on our recently cleared demonstration table. The bird chirped at me continually. We could not put the bird back into its' nest and the local rep working with me said the obvious; take it to the humane society so they can take care of it. I stubbornly decided that I knew better. I was on the way to the airport anyway, so why not stop at a food store and buy some eggs and milk, and bread to feed it? There happened to be a pet store adjacent to the supermarket and I bought some lice powder.
The cost was fifteen dollars. I was two and a half hours from home by air and the airport was beckoning. I packed the eggs etc. in a suitcase and put the bird in my coat pocket. The rep again said that the local animal shelter could do as well, but I said that I was bound and determined to see it through. He shrugged and drove me to the airport where I unloaded my suitcases and bid a fond farewell. I walked up to the counter to check in and at that moment the bird stuck his head out of my coat pocket and chirped loudly. The ticket agent then told me that there was a "bird fare" charge of thirty-five dollars. I paid the fee in cash and proceeded to the waiting area. The bird did not chirp the rest of the trip. I arrived at home and immediately drove to a pet store and purchased a small cage, cuttle bone and seed. The cost was thirty-eight dollars. The bird was freed a week later.
Simple math tells us that eighty-eight dollars was spent when logic dictated that the animal shelter was the best choice. Hindsight is truly twenty-twenty.

My mother decided to sell her dream home and move to Colorado to be close to family.
I was in Florida for a time working and I was ready to travel back to Chicago the next day. I stopped by to see my mother and she showed me a two-door freezer in her utility room. She then told me that she had a side of beef in the freezer. She opened the doors to the freezer and showed me a multitude of prime packaged meat. There were steaks of different cuts, rib roasts, briskets and more. There was one hundred and fifty pounds of frozen meat, rock hard, wrapped in butchers paper and saran wrap. She told me that she wanted to give me the entire lot at no charge. I had been traveling for a week and was short on sleep. The idea of all of that meat, my favorite cuts, free of charge made sense at the time, and Mom

always knows best. I accepted. I needed something to pack the meat in, so I drove down town to a hardware store and purchased four large insulated coolers priced at forty-five dollars each. I drove back to the house and began to load up the meat. The meat had to stay frozen, so I drove to an ice company and purchased a lot of dry ice, as well as stopping to buy a roll of duct tape to wrap the coolers on the way home. I said goodbye to mom and again thanked her for the meat. I then drove to the airport and then off loaded the coolers and returned the rental car. I had my big suitcases, my four coolers, and a clothing bag and my briefcase. The luggage clerk quickly informed me that my luggage was within limits and checked the bags through. The luggage clerk then informed me that the coolers needed to be sent by airfreight on the same flight. As luck would have it the freight office was on the other side of the airport property. I called a cab and one quickly appeared from the frontage road. The taxi driver smiled, opened his trunk and said, " Where is your luggage?" I responded by pointing to the four large tape covered coolers. The driver told me that his cab was too small to carry the coolers, and called for a station wagon. I paid the driver five dollars for his trouble. A large station wagon with the Yellow Cab logo drove into the loading zone and the driver and I loaded the coolers into the back.

"Where are you going?" he asked. I told him that I needed to go to the freight office across the airport. He informed me that a short haul like that took him away from a good long fare and that it would cost ten dollars each way. With flight time rapidly approaching I was too tired and too rushed to argue and we proceeded to the freight office, where I was told that the cost to ship the coolers was fifty-five dollars. I paid it and was driven back to the flight center. I paid the driver and barely made the flight. I was so tired that I tried to catch forty winks on the plane. The lesson with the taxi back at home was still percolating in my mind, so I called for a station wagon upon arrival at Chicago. The only thing that had gone right was the combined arrival of my luggage and the coolers together at the luggage counter. Also, a ten-dollar tip for the luggage clerk to get a cart to carry all of my stuff seemed to work very well. I was on a roll, I was almost home and the twenty-four dollar cab fare to my apartment was the crowning cost. I was exhausted yet elated. I off loaded and dragged the assemblage into my ground level apartment. To my surprise the tiny freezer on the top of the refrigerator was full and the awareness dawned on me that I did not have a freezer to put all of that frozen meat away.

Rather upset with myself for not remembering the obvious, I climbed into my car and bleary-eyed drove several miles to my neighborhood Sears store and waddled into the appliance department. A kind sales person approached me and I asked to see a freezer that was compact but would hold one hundred and fifty pounds of frozen meat. I was shown a tub freezer first and I said, "I'll take it!" The salesman smiled and told me of the backlog of deliveries that they had, and that they could deliver it the next business day.

I was tired, I was sleepy, and I was cross, but I did the right thing and asked to speak to a supervisor. I explained the quandary that I had found with the delivery arrangements and myself, and a price of three hundred and twenty five dollars was paid plus a delivery charge of fifty dollars for same day delivery. The wait for the delivery was stress beyond belief, I wanted it and I wanted it now. Celebration! The freezer arrived and I loaded the beast with the load of frozen meat. Total cost for the meat, more than my mother had paid for the meat by almost half. The irony, three weeks later I went on a three-week trip and came back to find that the power had been cut to the apartment due to blizzard conditions and all of the meat was ruined, and had to be thrown away. Nary a steak was eaten.

Note: The *lack of sleep, pressure, and stress cause the bipolar to turn to the manic. That just means that our minds are open to other options that the real world views as skewed. Psychotherapy really is the answer.*

I eventually had to quit work. I was in serious trouble, and credit card debt still ran neck and neck with health issues for a loss. My brother, who is a wonderful man, is married to a wonderful wife and has two great kids, came to my aid. He had to fly into Chicago from his home to spend four twelve-hour days to separate and trash all the assembled boxes. What an embarrassment. I am forever indebted to him for his help.

I have been in several hospitals for surgeries and also in several hospitals to balance diagnoses and medicines. I was 53 before the diagnosis of bipolar was made. I did not know about mania or depression, they were simply entries in the lexicon of life, something that other people had, not myself. I was living in denial. I went through several different medicines before the right one for me was found to work.

Am I nuts? Nope, just more of a realist than ever before.
You hear the terms, what do they mean: manic–depressive, bipolar1, bipolar2?
Lets look at them.

Symptoms of mania

Speeding thoughts
Buzzed all night, with little sleep
A rush
Happy, laughing, loud, euphoric
Angry, or irritated
Verbally combative
Risky behavior, flirting with disaster
Engaging in non-stop working, with no or very little sleep
Excessive spending
Varied or excess sexual liaisons
Drug use
Alcoholism
Thoughts about suicide
Forgetfulness

Overspending
Bad business choices
Grandiose ideas about our capabilities

Symptoms of depression

No get up and go
No will to live a social life
Crying and sadness that doesn't go away
Having guilt or feeling useless
Becoming disinterested in our normal lives
Irritation, even anger
Loss of memory
Inability to concentrate
Life loses meaning
Buy things to feel better
Become a couch potato
Stay in bed and sleep a lot
Loose a lot of sleep
Thoughts of death
Thoughts of suicide or death
Lost ability to make decisions

Manic-Depressive illness is now called Bipolar
Bipolar disorder is chronic
Bipolar disorder tends to be more common with women than men
Bipolar1 means serious mania and serious depression, episodes reoccur
Bipolar2 means less severe mania, and depression, or a milder form of mania called Hypomania alternating with depression
When several episodes occur in a year's time, it is said to be rapid cycling
Episodes may occur several times a day or several times a week
The older we get the rapid cycling tends to increase
Untreated, the manic and depressive occurrences become more severe
UNDERSTAND THIS!
BEING DIAGNOSED AND BEING TREATED IS NOT A CURSE.
WE ARE AT ONE WITH THE ILLNESS. IT IS PART OF US.

MANY OF THE WORLDS' MOST FAMOUS ARTISTS, MUSICIANS, SCULPTORS, AND CAPTAINS OF INDUSTRY, POLITICIANS AND JUST PLAIN OL' GOOD FOLKS ARE BIPOLAR.

THE GOOD NEWS IS—- there are several medicines that now exist to treat the disease:
Lithium and Depakote require blood tests to determine appropriate dosage levels.
Trileptal does not require frequent blood tests to determine appropriate dosage levels.
Tegretol is used as well.

REMEMBER! PSYCHOTHERAPY IS 50% OF HEALING
AND MEDICATION IS THE OTHER 50%.
Millions are affected by the problems symptomatic to bipolar. The bipolar disorder is hard to diagnose.

Comments to be wary of:

"You should know better."
"For crying out loud, you're supposed to be an adult."
"Look, it's mind over matter."
"Grow up."
"You should know how to handle money by now."
"Get over it."

Comments that mental health professionals should abolish:

"It is our opinion."
"How does/did that make you feel?"

A word about the Magic Ladder

DNA, the building blocks of life look like a twisted ladder. Their makeup dictates the physical traits of all that we are. It is genetics.

We, as human beings, exist as the sum total of generations of both sides of our families patterns back to square one. The simple truth is that if the DNA chains are not complete, according to plan or are missing factors, the being does not survive normally or does not survive at all. How many times have we heard "you look just like your father or mother?"

Or, "you look like your brother or sister." Or, "There is a family resemblance." It is the wonder of life, and the experience of it. The same qualities in nature that make all individuals different, seem to allow for a rule of thumb, and shall we say—for every inability there is an equal or stronger ability. Some abilities are natural and some are learned, and others developed.

A friend of mine is blind; but he has the most perfect hearing that I have ever run across. He can pick up a conversation twice as far as we, the sighted. The same holds true for those of us that are bipolar. Many of us are exceptional in some way—in music, art, jurisprudence, politics, business, public service and the list goes on and on for we are not alone in this illness and we are in very good company. If you believe that you are without talent, hearken to this—try writing, poetry, and art, music appreciation, stamp collecting, golf, try them all and more. Dollars to doughnuts you are darned good at something.

We of the bipolar, can track it back to childhood. Others develop the condition in the teens and the twenties. Adult crises may trigger the disorder as well. A personal traumatic experience or loss can generate the condition.

Thanksgiving Day

One of my best friends is a high fashion model. I was introduced to a life long friend of hers who was staying in Chicago at the time.

I decided to invite my new friend and her roommate to Thanksgiving dinner. I could not just purchase an already prepared turkey from the supermarket nearby, (The normal thing to do, in a rush), no, I had to make the stuffing and prepare the bird myself. My favorite meal was incomplete with just one bird for three people, so I put two 23-pound thawed turkeys, in my oven, around ten a.m. Both of the birds had a neat little thermometer that would pop up when they were done. My new friends arrived a bit early at eleven, bearing the gift of a bottle of fine wine. With introductions past, we all sat down in the living room to watch a rented movie and sipped wine and ate cheese, crackers, and fruit.

Five hours passed, and three movies later, we changed places on divan couch and chair to ease the minor aches and pains from sitting too long in one place. I had informed the ladies that the meal should be ready at three pm, but that was destined to be a mistruth.

Every time I had cooked a turkey, the time frame that was suggested was right on the money. I was tired from a long business trip the week before, and very rushed. My friends and I talked for an hour or so, and I decided to check the status of the birds.

To my dismay, the birds were just warm to the touch, and the thermometer had not budged. At five o'clock I decided to explain to my guests that my oven seemed to be laboring to cook the birds, so we settled on having peanut butter and jelly sandwiches, to stave our hunger. There is nothing better than fine Chablis wine, but not with peanut butter and jelly, I can attest. There was no milk because there was no room in the refrigerator; the thawing birds took up too much space. I could not leave my guests to purchase milk and a pre-cooked bird, of course not. That was a quandary I later pursued.

At seven pm the smell of cooking turkeys permeated the apartment, and our tummies were rumbling. Scents of sage, onion, garlic and cooking buttered turkey assailed our nostrils and we started to have a pool as to when the meal would be ready.

Keep in mind; these ladies earned a thousand dollars an hour as models, and they had infinite patience in front of the cameras and the crowds, but by ten pm their patience had worn thin. The smells were over powering; I peeked into the oven. Hurrah, the thermometer was half up and I saw a fine meal in the coming. By eleven pm the birds were done. All of us had to go to work the following day, and we were all exhausted by sensory overload. Delicate sensibilities were abraded. We decided to bring out my freezer quality quart and gallon Ziploc plastic bags. I loaded 10 bags full of sliced turkey, stuffing, and gravy and gave them to the ladies. They left for home shortly thereafter.

The final tally, three games of Monopoly, four rented movies, one and a half bottles of wine, four pbj's and good company for twelve hours. I was able to glean some of the turkey for a single sandwich. The balance went into bags and they were frozen. No Thanksgiving dinner that night. In reality, many things were overlooked. I look back and laugh, for it had not entered my mind to go to a restaurant and have an enjoyable dinner with the ladies, in fact most of the problems incurred were from not reading the instructions on the birds tags, and the fact that the oven was overtaxed with two turkeys. Besides, I was always right. Right! We seem to miss reality and follow our own star, even when others cannot even attest that it is there.

Bipolar Experiences

I mentioned the total devastation of my finances. I also spoke of my buying sprees.

Lest I not forget, buying penny stocks over the phone lost me thousands. The weird idea of buying them from a broker that I did not even know, and placing trust in, after letting me lose the money used the boiler room procedure of suckering the mark into another purchase, that had to be a big money maker. The first stock never got government authorization and went bust. And the second, well, the president of the firm spent all of the capital raised on wine, women, and song. Did I miss the loss of the money? I did not. It all blended into the process of my spending everything that I made on the most expensive goods. I bought a down comforter and pillows, all fine goose down and never put it on the bed. If money was spent, and I could not make payments due, I sold items just purchased at a loss. I was not in denial...I was out of control. My family just felt that I was no good with money, and that I spent it like water flowing through my fingers. Yet no one had any idea that I was mentally ill, and no one wanted to deal with that thought, I was not to be trusted with money. The danger resides in the fact that you get comfortable and the "stuff" seems to warm you into feeling that it all is normal; sure, everyone lives the same way too right? Nope!

In looking back, every time I had a surgery, or mental anguish, I started spending, big time! My performance in the workplace failed. I learned that mental anguish, as in a divorce or the loss of a loved one can trigger the bipolar disorder called late onset with adults, and early onset in youth. When my life was on the last legs of a journey to the poor house, I checked with a firm that offered to consolidate my bills as well as lower the interest on all of my 10 credit accounts, all full to the max. They quickly assessed my debts and quickly suggested that I declare bankruptcy. If I had a house I would have been able to lose it because a second mortgage would not be enough to cover my bills. As mentioned before, I lost my profit sharing, and my social life as well as my self-respect.

In today's world the debt consolidating firms say that you will save a whopping two hundred and fifty dollars a month by lowering interest. The credit card companies support some of those firms, and the fees you end up paying fund others.

If the truth were known, negotiating your principal down and canning all or part of the interest, seems like a pipe dream, it is not. The credit card companies would rather get some money, rather than none in a bankruptcy. The Debtors Anonymous folks can help. They can tell you where the meetings are, and help you through the tough times by teaching you at many meetings, that many folks in all walks of life are there to recover and to mentor.

Contact information will be supplied at the end of the book.

I had heard of the horrors of psych wards. Did I think that I would ever be in the same?

No. Yet when the time came for me to be put under those circumstances, I found a lot of kind people in the process of drug balancing, and with a lot of support and the people around me worked hard to get back into society. Times have changed and mental health specialists are pouring out of colleges with the latest known of progress, and method. The world of mental health care has changed, much to the better. Many of us may go to hospitals for treatment, and some will have two or more stays in hospitals as well.

It is time to tell you about the problems that arise when other disorders couple with bipolar disorder.

As a child I always had a voice with me. I never told anyone about it and it bothered me more as I got older. I found that the voices I heard presented themselves because I had schizoid-affective disorder in concert with bipolar disorder with psychotic features.

Voices, like whispers in the night. Full conversations with grand offers to peak the imagination occurred with me. I am going to list a lot of hours long discussions with my voices, and the truths about the disorder that I found later.

Firstly, sounds like a car passing, the hum of an air conditioner, the running of a faucet the blowing of air through a fan, the wind, all associated in my mind to form words. Even shuffling papers equate to words. Surrealistic? You bet.

I found myself almost sure that I was losing my mind. Then I started to think, actually hearing myself think. Right. I could think of a phrase loudly and in scanning left to right or right to left with my eyes seconds later a whisper/read form of communication took place. We are told that to every action there is a reaction. Well, I learned to sign with a new communication that utilized my fingers to spell words at high speed.

I suddenly found that I could hear a song and tap the different beats, voice, bass, and sax riffs at different tempos, each finger tapping separate beats. I learned a form of relaxing to music, and losing myself to the music. Hence we come to the statement "I don't just march to the beat of different drummer, I'm the whole band." All true.

I spent hours talking back and forth with the voices and only one thing proved to be my salvation. I had seen the movie "A Beautiful Mind", and had read the book as well.
Later I found something that would prove to be a key answer for me and tell me that I was a giant amongst men, or not. Later, as it happened, I found that the voices were all the same, no inflection; all the same even the whispers sounded the same. This fact helped. When I was diagnosed as bipolar and schizoid-affective answers began to form.
The feeling is a bit hard to explain, I will give it a go.
I hear voices; they are behind my right ear or behind me or in the air as in a distant radio broadcast, yet it is in my mind. Not outside, but inside my head. I would think, "I need to get up from my chair". But a voice would whisper, "You have been sitting there too long". The voices seemed to beat me up, or sometimes raise me to the heights.
It is no wonder that children become scared with the same condition. Make no mistake, I am getting better, and the good news is that you can too.

I will give you a few samples of the grand plans and meetings I have had with world figures:

I have a transmitter lodged in my gold crown in my mouth.
I am able to communicate by just thinking.
I teach others to communicate with their minds.
I am called the General.
I have been promoted to the Joint Chiefs of Staff.
I am being named as the Commanding General of the Air Force.
I am able to promote friends to high ranks in the military.
I am the White House Chief of Staff.
I am the head of the Secret Service.
I am the director of the National Security Agency.
I talk with The President of The United States.
The Vice President is my mentor.
I speak to the Pope through a translator.
I speak with the Prime Minister of England.
I can bring peace to the Middle East.

I am the Ambassador to the British Isles.
I am the White House Press Secretary.
I am the Commanding Officer of a special Psi corps of the military.
I am the phantom airman, saving aircraft in distress.
I speak to the Apollo/Soyuz space station.
I can throw my mind to Venus, and it bounces back.

The list goes on for pages. It sure took a patch of time for each marathon conversation!

You see, the sum total of what I know, all facts, all that I read, all that I saw on television, read in magazines, in science fiction books, non fiction, the sum total of my mind seemed to present itself not at my command, but unbidden. I found myself thinking to myself rather than talking. Isolation began. I would think a simple sentence, but the voice would respond by waxing eloquent. You may ask how does one survive without going crazy? Well, meds, a basic working knowledge of mental health by living it, and ideas provided by mental health specialists. Counseling helped, so did the Internet, and the love and affection of my family helps as well.

The extreme changes in mood, to anger, to euphoria to depression, are hallmarks of the bipolar mind. Remember, over two million Americans are bipolar. Years may pass before they are correctly diagnosed. The bipolar disorder begins slowly in appearance, but it reappears more and more the older that we get. It may last for years, or a lifetime.

The disorder may present itself in hours, a day, months or years, without rhyme or reason. It can be a curse if we let it become one, but it can be tolerated and understood and that is our shield. This is job one.

Some say, " he or she has a very bad temper, or he or she laughs without control, or he or she seems to be very sad a lot of the time." Many different forms of mental illness have been discovered and the bipolar condition may be hard to tell from other disorders and it is not labeling, it is grounding. Many of us, the bipolar, need hospital stays to balance us and to heal. Medicines must be tried.

Depression ranks twice as much in women, as in men. The workplace suffers because of tardiness, failure to be able to work, or working at a reduced rate of production.

Is this our fault? No it is not. The fact that you are reading this book is a major first step towards healing and survival.

The Surgeon General has stated that mood disorders rank among the top ten causes of worldwide disability. Think of the numbers! 44 million in the United States alone.

It took me three years to find the right balance of medicines and to start to heal.

If things could go wrong, they did. The shakes, the loss of hair, the severe drop in white blood cell count plagued me. It does not mean that you will be affected the same way.

Be of good cheer. Look, all we have is time, and your doctor has tests that can quickly determine if a med is good or bad for you, but take time to let the meds work.

I cannot stress enough the fact that the input to our doctors, psychologists, and mental health specialists is required and the honesty in our reporting them is most necessary.

Talk to them. Treatment is a saving grace; do not fail to get help. The earlier that we are diagnosed, the better and faster treatments can be found and our healing begins.

We must tell all to our health professional, and what is said is private and there is much comfort in that fact.

The major opinion is that a chemical imbalance in the brain is causative to the bipolar disorder. Other schools of thought parallel the bipolar disorder to epilepsy. Many drugs that were designed to help other disorders concerns seem to have good effects when used in the bipolar disorder. Different meds are for different folks. We are all different, so are our needs in treatment. Mental illness in the United States, (as discussed earlier) involves millions. All races, creeds, and religions are affected. The numbers are staggering, and growing with younger people being diagnosed. Depressive disorders, mild depression, bipolar, schizophrenia, obsessive compulsive, panic, anxiety, eating problems, ADHD and many others need to be treated by professionals.

One important factor involved with bipolar disorder, schizophrenia, and psychotic features is, that brushes with the law are common, some with terrible consequences.

The loss of life due to suicide is staggering, and symptomatic with us, and teenage suicides tell the tale that mental health issues are very common with them, with many being unresolved, as well as with adults and with children.

Keep guns and ammunition out of the house.

Be careful and do not imbibe in alcoholic beverages, they do not agree with our meds, and in the case of the undiagnosed, major mood changes can occur. I.e.: the mad drunk.

Over twenty eight thousand suicides happen each year, and the great majority were found to have mental illness.

The lack of understanding that anything is wrong with our actions leads us along the path to disaster. Even the mighty fall to the mistakes that are typical to our mental issues.

The stress on our families is unbelievable. The mental scars that are formed in response to our actions can only be healed by love and understanding, but some relationships are destroyed without any hope of repair.

NOTE: You will find that I repeat several points throughout this book. These repetitions are with intent.

Antitransubstantial materialism

(A Word to those that cannot understand mental illness.)

Can you understand the above listed word? It may mean something but it is difficult to understand or comprehend. Mental illness may be just as hard for you to spell out, understand, or cope with.

You may never have had a sick day in your life, and you are hale and healthy.

You find yourself in a quandary when a mate, a child, a fellow worker, an employee, or an acquaintance, is found to have a mental disorder. If your every instinct tells you to cut the strings of that relationship, stop that thought right now.

It may just be the discomfort and fear of understanding that is affecting you.

You must rise above your discomfort and understand that a well-founded relationship is based on respect, or confidence, or affection or love. Pick which of these gifts apply to you and ask yourself if they should be cut asunder. There is a better way. Look forward to dealing with and learning all that you can about the disorder manifesting itself in us.

It is tough to fight off those negative feelings, but that is where job one comes into effect.

This is the real truth—You have to look at it all as an important job, one that must be done. It is not only the responsibility that must be shouldered, but also extending a helping hand to a person in need. A great part of the healing happens to be your support.

It gives us strength to go down a road to recovery. You are an integral part to the equation.

Remember, it has been said, "What man has done, man can do."

You are not alone in this effort. There are support groups for husbands, wives, children, and even the guardians of the work place. The Internet is a fine source of support sites for you. There are many support meetings in cities that you can attend and council with folks that share your issues and learn from those that have found the answers.

There are a myriad books on the market that deal with your issues, seek them out.
These commitments to support us are life issues for us.
You must take it on faith that you have the power to help, and that your help and support can do much, not just for recovery, but regaining the relationships that were temporarily weakened.
It is in your hands, you must be equal to the task. And you know what? A feeling of comfort and accomplishment will be yours.
Please know that in truth, you have needs regarding these issues too, a healing for both is side by side, in truth pairs.
You are capable of incredible good, and you have a strength inside of you that is called compassion.
Do the right thing, help. You may even identify it as "buying in to it".
In all rights, your acceptance of the fact that you can help is a work of grace.
Funnel your strengths, be a parent that listens, be a person that councils and supports your employees, be a mate that knows now how to deal with the affairs of the heart, or be an older sibling that agrees to unconditional love and understanding.
These are the works that will even save lives, have no doubt.
Do the right Thing, make the right choices, and join in the healing.

Living as Bipolar

We feel as if we know it all and we are willing to defend that position to the death.

The same visage as the teen that refuses the council of his/her parents, saying, "you don't know what I feel." Or, "You don't understand me," slamming the bedroom door in a fit.

Life is somewhat of a frustration considering that our mood swings are assumed to be normal. Issues become the fodder of mania, and giving up, the onus of depression.

Loved ones show frustration, and may fail to understand those feelings until educated.

That, by the way, is the only way to battle the issues that arise in our families.

It is difficult for a parent, husband, wife or sibling to understand the total depression that leaves us exhausted, staying in bed, or on the couch. When we are greeted by comments like "why don't you get up, or get out of bed." We may just roll over and ask the world to go away, or switch to mania yelling just leave me alone, or causing pain to our loved ones with sharp comments that burn the ears upon hearing. We do not understand that we cause pain in those we love, and often cannot know why someone has a hurt registering on their face because of our comments.

When frustrated, we are at a loss for words at times, and may become irritated or angry, and other times just give up. When pressured, we may mouth a word or idea that is not correct, and we feel added irritation because we know that we said the right thing, but cannot understand why it was not clear to the recipient.

Weight gain or loss is the partner to the mood issues, and we may binge, or starve just to make a point. But the echo of "I want it and I want it now" becomes reality to us.

Over spending is a common problem. Kids through adulthood can hang on to every penny, and still have everything because they can plan to the future. We live for the moment and without planned record keeping, we cannot keep up on our spending habits. Money seems to disappear and the problem comes to a head with disastrous financial consequences. The enemy is the ATM card, and the checkbook. The ATM is handy, we pull out the max allowed, and it is gone before it registers in our minds. The checkbook is a problem because we draw the cash out and the account is short come bill paying time.

We max out our credit cards, and strive to have the credit limits raised; yet we are astounded when we get the monthly bill, and can't remember what we bought.

We are sometimes in Grandiosity. We must be the big man on campus, and we buy the dinners out for friends or ply family and friends with gifts, regardless of their costs.

Both costs. Why both costs? One, we hide the fact that we are deep in debt and cannot afford to have the largesse. Two, the cost of embarrassment to our loved ones arises because they cannot respond in kind.

One day I spent a thousand dollars on a gift for my brother. I was amazed that he responded by looking frustrated, and with tears of hurt forming in his eyes he said, "I cannot afford to spend this kind of money for a gift to you, and don't you know that a simple card would do?" I was floored, and being the big man I said that it didn't matter, it is of no concern to me. Was that the right thing to say? Well, I thought so that at the time, but today I see that it was like pouring gasoline on the fires of pain in my brothers' eyes!

He and his family have put up with more frustration from me than I can list in five chapters, but they know that I am always trying to improve, the help coming from therapy and good med balancing. I love them madly. No pun!

I look at the broken bodies of my life, failure at business, the inability to rejoin society, no significant other, and the list go on and on. Am I depressed about it? No. Loving family, treatment and a good understanding of the mood issues, leads me to celebrate life, not give in to it.

We hear things differently, and may say things or grasp the inane and have different values when we are at our worst. To explain: and this is really making a little fun but it proves a point.

Mania is not a state in New England.
Delusional is not a major rainstorm.
Depression is not pushing all the buttons. No double meaning!
Psychotic is not a science fiction term of mind control or an old movie.
ADHD is not a license plate on the car of the leader of an advertising agency.
Unipolar is not either the South Pole or the North Pole.
Disorder is not unruly crowds.
Denial is not a river in Egypt.

We see the concept our own way, but cannot voice the right words when under stress.

Pivotal points in a life leave only tearful memories if we are in Mania or Depression.

We will bend, stamp, fold, and mutilate just to get by issues and to get the right result—what we want, right now.

Now, a few words about the balance of it all.

I have outlined some of the symptoms of the Bipolar/Unipolar condition. There are better and worse. There are many more nuances to the mind, but don't be dismayed.

It is like the color blind, they learn the different colors and act on that knowledge and education and lead their lives. We can do the same.

Try to see the kindness, humor, love, and the joy of life that that can be and should be yours. I say try, try again. Get treatment, medicines and make your doctor visits. You will succeed.

I believe that I have the following facts straight:

Abraham Lincoln ran for the Senate two times and the Congress once and lost each time. Disconsolate at the losses, he still prevailed and two years later was elected to the presidency of the United States of America. Lincoln had other successes in his life and career previous to the presidency. He was one of us. Be of good cheer.

More on Medicines Used

Remember, some of these drugs are for the children, some for adults.
Many of them are used for other disorders.
Your doctor may order a mixture of these drugs to deal with multiple symptoms.

(Remember to research your child's meds or your meds on the NIH web site: **www.Medlineplus.gov), research them well!**

The following drugs are in common use by doctors for bipolar disorder, as well as psychotic features and or schizoid concerns.

Anti-anxiety drugs for adults and children:
Ativan
Buspar
Klonopin
Xanax

There are different schools of thought as to the treatment of the bipolar condition.
One specifies channel blockers for extreme mood disorders:
Isradipine
Nimodipene
Verapamil

Another school specifies anticonvulsants.
Gabitril
Lamictal
Neurontin
Tegretol
Topamax

Another mood stabilizer is Lithium.

Lithium is an anti-suicidal drug, and is the granddaddy of the drugs listed.

Anti-psychotics are ordered for patients for hearing voices, visual and other delusions:
Risperdal
Zyprexa
Seroquil

Your mental health specialist will fill you in on the needs for your recovery.

Be sure to ask your doctor and pharmacist if any food interactions exist for the medications prescribed.

A quick word on the formula for the recovery of adults, children and adolescents.

The school environment must be a healthy one. Work with your child's teachers and give them the web site **www.bpkids.org** and have them look on the left column of the home page for the educators' information.
Spend some time reading the information for parents on that site yourself; it has a wealth of ideas and facts in well-written form.

How Depression Affects Us

Depression and major depression take a terrible toll on us. Life changes for the worse. The depression may become overwhelming, and sadness, tears, malaise, and frustration take over our lives and mute the health and goodness out of them. Our families, personal relationships and job performance are stressed, far beyond anything that we are aware of.

We can shut down, retreating to our beds, losing our self-image, and any vestige of our self-respect. Life becomes an unending blur, and we become lost.

The damage is insidious. It robs us of joy, and poisons our outlook. Untold values are lost. We can loose our desire for sex, suffer anguish, and even digestive illnesses become possible. We may overeat; gain weight, or loose weight by starving ourselves because we just give up. Life just sours.

Relationships can end, our kids or mate cannot understand what is happening, but know something is wrong.

There are no bounds for the variables in depression, we may know that something is wrong, but we are often clueless to the reasons for the changes that we go through. The tears, fears, and concern tap our strength and may embitter us.

There is more suicide involved in depression than we can possibly imagine, with men commiting suicide four times more often than women, although many women try.

Suicides occur from youth to the aged. The reason may be as simple as not knowing what to do. The terrible quandary is that if those who attempt to, or those that succeed had a glimmer that their lives could be bettered by professional counseling, medicines, with hospitals tailored to help their problems, and support groups, all with their health as their mission, the statistics could plummet and untold lives could be saved.

The message of these truths must be known, families educated and more information on hot lines made available. Action must be taken.

Depression is a complex and serious problem. Decisions may have to be made by families to turn it over to the professionals, we may go for help ourselves, or friends and clergy support us to make the right choices. The right of it is that medical attention and treatment works with a majority of us, and we deserve that peace as a voyage back to a healthy and happy life.

For the Parents

Many millions of children and teens have mental illnesses in our country.
Major depressive disorder, dysthimic disorder, and bipolar disorder are found in these children and adolescents. (Please go to the web site of the National Institute of Mental Health at **http://nimh.nih.gov** and look up " Brief notes on the Mental Health Of Children") Both NIMH and NIH are government web sites that can be of great importance to you as parents.
Bipolar disorder is difficult to diagnose in children and adolescents.
Bipolar disorder is a mood disorder, and there are anxiety disorders and attention deficit disorders as well.
ADHD disorder and bipolar disorder share some points of diagnosis.
A million or more children were moved from the diagnosis of ADHD to a diagnosis of bipolar disorder last year.
ADHD is more evident in male children than female children.
Psychotic or schizoid features may tag along with bipolar disorder.
In all cases:
Talk to your child's doctor, look up information on the web, go to your library, and learn about your child's problems, symptoms, and learn how to cope. Provide unconditional love to your child, the road to comfort and healing is captained by you. Make sure that you let the little one or adolescent know that you are there for them, and hugs, reassurance and understanding are the hallmark of healing. You may be surprised at the positive response. Are you up to it? Yes, when you understand that your efforts will be rewarded. Your support is so needed, because the family's support is a large part of healing to your children.
Take interest in your child's school performance, and help them get by the concerns of their homework, pay attention to their needs and congratulate them on their successes.
Children look up to their parents. It may not be evident to you, but you are the heroes and heroines to your children.

The Bipolar child and adolescent may tend to be one to his or her self. This isolation is not healthy to healing, but you can help by being a parent and friend, and suggesting peer relationships to your children at school, and at play.

Avoiding homework, telling mistruths about completing homework, drawing dark or bizarre pictures, fighting at school and a surly attitude, are symptoms of the bipolar child. Be calming, and look into those pained eyes and tell your kids that it will be all right. They need this reassurance.

Introduce the idea of going to a doctor for help.
Tell your child that you will be with him/her and that medicine will help.
Once the doctors' visit is over and your child has been given the daily medicine (if needed), be sure that no doses are skipped.
Use the websites and go to <u>links</u> to find more pertinent information.
<u>Please be aware that your child may need to try two or three different meds, one at a time, to find which is best tolerated. It may take months to find the right one.</u>
<u>Be of good cheer, it all is positive action to help your child back to health.</u>

Mental health is as important as it can be. If your child is involved in sports, band thespians etc. explain that good mental health should be as important as them all. The bipolar child requires mental activity, lots of it, so advise your child to get involved in sports, read, watch <u>some</u> television, (TV must be metered to provide the right programs.)

Pay attention to your child, reinforce your love and explain to the child that hearing voices, or noises in the night, will be okay, and you will be there for him/her. Tell the child that their thoughts are speeding and some of those thoughts are all it is. Hugs help.
Be sure to tell your child if the behavior is good or bad, this honesty helps reinforce the relationships of children to parents.

Your bipolar child is the product of genetics; it is no ones' fault.
Nothing could have changed the outcome, but the odds are that the child will have amazing talents in some area.
You will be amazed when your child is on the path to healing.

Speak to your child's teachers, share your knowledge, ask your kid's mental health professional to call the school, if needed and speak to the nurse or social worker.

Share some of the web sites with them as well.

Privacy, anonymity and kindness are benchmarks of these issues of which we speak.

You must share your words and feelings with the children. Come to an understanding about mental health issues and look to your doctor for help.

The Children

Bipolar disorder in children is hard for moms and dads to accept.

So many things went perfectly, a beautiful baby, loveable, and everything the proud parents wanted.

No one could have warned the parents of a mood disorder in their children.

Let me stress a point right now: You did nothing "wrong" at all.

The wonders of genetics were in play. They are a legacy that we cannot ignore. The engineering of the human body is garnered from sources that we, at this time cannot change. However the symptoms can be treated. In years to come we can look forward to a cure and healing, for the medical breakthroughs are coming forward fast and furiously.

Areas such as the Omega-3 concentrated oils are being prescribed by psychiatrists around the country as a partner to normal medicines already in use. Many more answers will be forthcoming.

(Be sure to keep in touch with the "News" section found daily on **www.MedlinePlus.gov**). Also, please avail yourselves of the Kids Health website, **www.kidshealth.org** Lots of answers are found there.

Anger in the child, sometimes destructive, problems in school, and a penchant for mistruths, with cycling anger and depression occurring many times every day, leads parents to the sharp edge of worry and concern. Dismal times in the child heralding depression are hard to deal with but they are treatable. Depression can take a terrible toll. Child suicide has increased each year in the last five charted. I watched a bipolar child grow up. Instant rage, instant depression is noticed in the child, yet there are times when the child is "just fine." The attention deficit concerns that were the subject of many news articles telling us that many children that were diagnosed with ADHD now herald the fact that a number of the children are being diagnosed as bipolar.

A million or so of these children now are engaged in the diagnosis of bipolar 1 and depression. These kids need comforting, love, support, hugs and understanding.

As parents we cannot handle this alone. We must get our kids to a child psychiatrist, get a course of treatment, and set up counseling. This is a must do.

Why did so many diagnoses of our children change? Both disorders are similar in like symptoms yet they each support different medications and treatment.
Some symptoms in the bipolar child may be as simple as, "Mom or Dad, I have a headache and my tummy hurts, I can't go to school today." This is heard, time after time. Homework just cannot get done, and other symptoms occur.
Sometimes these issues must be addressed in a firm manner. Yes, your pediatrician can put you in contact with a child psychiatrist, for the much needed meds and council. Be honest with your doctor ask any and all questions until you are fully informed as how to deal with your child and the bipolar disorder.
You will have privacy in all rights.
Bias and stigma are part of the great misunderstanding of mental health. Some people are still having the opinion that, "You don't talk about those problems," or "Other people have those problems, not my family."
This kind of denial can be hazardous to the bipolar child's health. Many school nurses, social workers and teachers are learning about the bipolar disorder and can be a support for your child. Mental health is one of the most important issues of our times. Make no mistake. Kids are to be cherished, and the good news is the treatment that has helped many a child, and can do so with yours. Your child can grow up more knowledgeable, and grow up to be a great mom or dad. Remember, the miniature electric waterfalls that are found in many stores are great to have around the house. The sound of falling rain and bubbling brooks can be of great comfort to your bipolar child. They are great stress reducers for adults too. Your child may require one or more medicines during the balancing of his or her needs in treating their bipolar disorder. Medicines must be tried, balanced and adjusted. Thyroid medicines may be needed.
Have no fear; your childs' doctor will have everything well in hand.
Please refer to the NIH and follow the sites that you find on Medline plus under health topics, type in bipolar, and get ready to research and educate yourselves for the sake of your children.

To the Adolescent

The whole world is your oyster, right? How do you feel, can you conquer tomorrow?

You have reached the point in your life when the important things are, going to school, dating, getting that drivers' license, driving your folks' car or your own, possibly a part time job, hobbies, and the library and more. Is everything perfect? Or not.

Life may be hard to swallow, anger come unbidden, or all of the time. Sadness and tears may be a continuous problem as well as concentration. In truth the teen with bipolar disorder or depression called unipolar, is a respondent to a childhood filled with their parents concern, just as they are concerned about you today.

You might have been bipolar as a baby or in childhood. Bipolar disorder can appear in the teen years as well. Is it a curse? No way! Can you be treated for it? Yes! Can the bipolar disorder be cured? Not at this time, but major strides in medicine, treatment, and research are being made every day. Besides that, you have a gift. You have not yet touched the genius inside of you.

Bipolar one and bipolar2 and unipolar are mood disorders. Bipolar disorder manifests itself in children, teens and adults. It is caused by a traumatic experience and the environment in our young lives, that changes us, and the way we perceive life. Bipolar 1 disorder is a real and complex medical illness; symptoms entail extreme changes in our moods, our energies, and how we act. Our moods cycle between real highs to the depths of depression. Then we have periods of time with no symptoms at all. We experience the bipolar disorder through our lives. Many of us have the disorder as teens, and many teens are untreated. The symptoms are similar to ADHD and other disorders and is difficult to treat.

Many of the untreated may live with bipolar disorder for several years without treatment.

You can read more about them through this book.

Besides that, you and I have some talking to do!

Look, the symptoms are about the same as an adult, mania and depression or unipolar depression. Deep depression may be our lot, keeping is in it's lock Do not despair. Every one has the good times, and some depression from time to time, we are a little different.

Let's look at a few symptoms that may apply to you, and help you identify what is happening in your life right now.

I can do things better than others, attitude
Sadness, crying depression
Can't seem to get out of bed
Moody
Extreme desires for sweets and carbohydrates
Terror filled dreams
Distain or defiance towards adults, parents, or teachers
Non-stop activity
Racing thoughts
Having trouble concentrating
Excess dating with improper choices in sex
Seeing things that others cannot
Hearing voices
Extreme anger or irritation
Making poor choices in life
Thoughts of suicide
Lack of sleep
Overspending
Speeding thoughts
Can't do anything right

These are some of the symptoms of the bipolar disorder, mania and depression. They are all treatable, and with counseling and medicines we can address life and go on with our lives. It takes commitment and work but you can do it!

You know that we give a lot of grief to our parents, because we know better. Right?

Let me give you a quote attributed to Mark Twain. That's right, the Huck Finn guy.

"When I was a boy of fourteen, my father was so ignorant that I could hardly stand to have the old man around. But when I got to be twenty one, I was astonished at how much the old man had learned in seven years." <u>Embrace this concept.</u>

Many times we are moody to the point that we loose friends, or seek the wrong crowd.

Do you think that you are significant in your disorder? Get by that, life has too much to offer, and you are in very good company, you already have the ticket.

Again, do you give your parent or parents a ration of lip, arguing, knowing that you are right and they are wrong? This is a teen thing first, but we the bipolar take it a good bit farther.

You are already asking yourself if there is any good news to the concept of the bipolar disorder thus far in these pages. Yes there is.

I am going to digress from the format to tell you about a number of fine people that have what you and I have, an ability that we could not see but for the trees, until we were informed or discovered it, and suddenly it dawns on us that these abilities were untapped.

We heal through treatment, medicines and education. What really helps is our knowing that there are people out there past and present that have lived our problems and triumphed over them.

Some of the best books to read about our disorder have been written by Kay Redfield Jamison.

Kay Redfield Jamison is an American psychologist and science writer who is affected by manic depression, also known as bipolar disorder. She is internationally known and is currently a Professor of Psychiatry at the Johns Hopkins School of Medicine.

Kay Redfield Jamison and Frederick K Goodwin wrote "Manic-Depressive Illness" one of the classic textbooks on the bipolar disorder.

Doctor Jamison's' works include:

"An Unquiet Mind" (autobiography) ISBN0679763309

Touched with Fire: Manic-Depressive Illness and the Artistic Temperament" (1993) (Includes a study of Lord Byron's illness), ISBN068483183X

"Night Falls Fast": Understanding Suicide", ISBN037570148

Jamison is the recipient of the National Mental Health Association's William Styron Award (1995), The American Suicide Foundation Research Award (1996), The Community Mental Heal Leadership Award (1999), and is a 2001 MacArthur Fellowship recipient. And more!

Remember, you have an ability that will flower if you educate yourself about our disorder, get treatment, find your peace with family and friends and strengthen your self-image and coping skills. We need help in this. A professional must help us with our fears, priorities, coping skills and our individual needs. We have things to say.

Now, lets meet some of the people that lived or are living with our disorder. As a mental exercise look some of them up, ask your folks, ask your teacher, check your library, and write in below each name, who and what they are or were. This is not homework, and it is not wasted effort. This is part of the awakening of that genius, and expanding your mind,

Hans Christian Anderson
William Faulkner
F. Scott Fitzgerald
Samuel Clemens (Mark Twain)
Ralph Waldo Emerson
Charles Dickens
Herman Melville
Patty Duke (Be sure to read her book on her bipolar experience).
Axl Rose
Charley Pride
Ted Turner
Jonathon Winters
Robert Louis Stevenson
Stephen Foster
Robert Schumann
Charles Ives
Gustav Holst
Robert Burns
Cole Porter
Kurt Cobain
Paul Gaugin
Vincent van Gogh
Victor Hugo
James Russell Lowell
Boris Pasternak
Edna St. Vincent Millay
Dylan Thomas
Walt Whitman

Michelangelo Buonarroti (You know, the Sistine Chapel)
Thomas Gray
Robert Frost
Hermann Hess
Dick Cavett
Peter Gabrial
Kristy McNichols
Buzz Aldren
Eric Clapton
Sheryl Crowe
Michael Critchton
Anthony Hopkins
Sarah McLachian
Roseanne
James Taylor

That's right, they all rose above their disorders to greater achievements, just as we can! Now friends, we must discuss one very serious fact, some of these people committed suicide, by the way, that does not mean that you will.

It's a factor in young lives as well. Suicides happen in all age groups, from children to the aged.

Teens have a lot of stresses. Life itself, peer pressure, academic pressure, and important issues that impact them daily and from the past, their environment, and hormones make for a rather delicate mix. If coping skills are not present, if we don't know what to do, if we are deeply depressed, all avenues available to us seem to be shut, and we don't know how to get help or from whom, to seek that help.

Possible symptoms of major depression can be thoughts of death and even thoughts of suicide. If you or a friend ever has these issues, seek help. Just think, "I can't handle this, but someone else can." Talk to your parents, call your church, talk to your school nurse, your doctor or in the gravest extreme pick up the phone and **call 1-800-Suicide.** Use local suicide hot lines as well. Talk it out. Too many promising young lives are snuffed out when despair has taken over and we seem to have lost our way.

The most traumatic thing to happen to our folks is to lose a child. Our friends are affected, and depressed, our teachers suffer the loss as well, our teammates cannot understand, but they are sad and disrupted.

People that we could not imagine caring are impacted.

Teen drinking and using drugs is part of the element, so is the anger that pushes teens to take risks and make bad choices and decisions driving motor vehicles.

The teen, by age twenty, may have heard about, or know a person that died this way.

The statistics on teen deaths are higher than you could imagine.

The teens that are untreated for the bipolar disorder or depression may have poor grades in school or a sudden drop in scholastic success. And can even be argumentative when faced with the realities by teachers and parents.

We will always find an excuse for our problems, believe me, I did.

The changes in the body as we grow to adulthood are fodder enough to cause stress or some depression. By the way, sleeplessness, stress, high sugar and more can make the bipolar person's health much worse. Learn to calm yourself down, learn yoga or tai chi.

Practice the process of deep breathing from the stomach (watch a baby breathe, that tummy goes up and down as it breathes"). We tend to chest breath when we become stressed. Get engaged in exercise, walk, it all helps our depression and anger get better, and helps us cope.

Teens are susceptible to depression, as we discussed earlier, sometimes deep depression leaves us mixed up to the point where we cannot stand it any more. If you ever begin to feel this way, fight it. Go to your parents ask to discuss it and ask them to see your doctor. Show them what you have researched on teen and adult bipolar disorder and depression. Most parents love their children and are happy to find out what you are feeling, and to help you deal with it. Go to church, read up on all bipolar literature that you can, and surf the web for bipolar adolescent and kids. There are tons of good comforting articles and personal stories, as well as a lot of organizations and government agencies that stand to educate you.

If you are troubled, this is what you should do. Go to your family doctor or clinic with a parent there for support. Get an exam and possibly a blood draw to make sure your thyroid function is not too high or too low. It is a good idea to have your blood sugar count checked as well. Get a copy of all medicines that you are taking and get a copy of your medical history. Get a referral to a psychiatrist or mental health therapist.

You will begin a process of stress reduction, have a professional to talk to you about your individual issues, and begin some form of medication and a lot of recovery to make life a joy not a hassle or drudge. Let's be truthful, if you are out of control, and you need concentrated care, a short hospital stay may be necessary. This is a healthy thing, just like you might go to the hospital for medical help with a broken bone and some recovery is needed to make you right. We need special care to reestablish a balance, salve what ails us, strengthen our resolve, help us to deal with our personal issues and to get advice on life.

Be truthful to your folks and to your doctor, and be honest with yourself.

Life, as you will find, is a delicate balance of wonderment and reality, but your eyes must be open to it to embrace it.

Please know that you do not have a diseased mind, you are not mental, nuts, crazy, or out of your mind. As a matter of fact, bipolar teens are intelligent people, and with treatment and therapy we gain an education and more control of our lives than most.

Why get care? Sometimes our peers mistreat us because of our unorthodox ways.

We do not recognize the totally rational view because we are so involved with our selves.

We want the sometimes unattainable, "I want it and I want it now." Is heard, loud and clear.

This may pertain to parental love and attention, use of the family car, dating habits, and possibly even a closet full of clothes that you rarely use. We may buy a lot of stuff mishandle our money, and the pressures at school can feed all of this.

We are slaves to the issues until we seek help, take the meds, read up on it, and practice.

The concepts that help us ease the patterns of our bipolar disorder. This is maintaining a life that flowers to a bright future, yours.

As we have seen, artists and people of note have lived through their lives even with the bipolar disorder manifesting itself in them every day. It should not be a burden; it is part of what made them excel at their crafts. It is at one with them.

You see the fame, the good life or the ordinary stands as part and parcel of your future.

Can you see the wonder of it all? We have been given a gift, not a curse. The bipolar condition is part of us. Well tempered, it is a sunrise of immense proportion.

We are blessed with talents and genius. You must fulfill the destiny of your life.

I am going to ask you to visit some of the web sites listed in the back of the book. Search through them, pick the best of them, download copies and file them for review.

Learn, and pass it on, you may just save a life down the road.

Lock, Stock and Barrel

I have spoken to several people with bipolar parents in families of four to five.
In all cases, bipolar parents that birthed the sons and daughters, one or two of the progeny were bipolar 1 or bipolar 2.
Several were unipolar with female members of families having severe depression, yet fewer males were unipolar. (These facts were rendered from interviews, and may not hold true in all cases, but statistics show the genetic legacy to be so).

As I mentioned earlier in the book, my fathers' family had three brothers and two sisters.
Two of the brothers were bipolar and another was ill of severe depression.
The sisters and one brother did not have the bipolar disorder.
My father told me that his father was a calm man with a modest temper. His mother had a bad temper. My father mentioned to me once that his mother, irritated at two of the brothers, chased them around the kitchen of their home with a carving knife. The brothers took it as an inside joke years later. My father and one uncle had bipolar disorder, but many years passed before the bipolar factor became readily identified. The issue was, both being in the medical field themselves, they had no idea that any one with a temper, or blue days had a problem. Besides, they once said to me, "The only people with mood issues were other doctors involved with that healing."
The process of visiting a psychiatrist in those days was secretive, and of course the denial of something they did not know about made it a non-issue.
Keep in mind, when, as a child I was taken to see a psychiatrist, and the fellow had to be two hundred and fifty miles away, to make sure no one noticed it.

As mentioned, my father was bipolar. I am bipolar. My brother is not bipolar.
My brothers' oldest son, not bipolar, but his younger brother is.
The truth told, the bipolar or unipolar legacy is just being found to be the tip of the iceberg of mood and anxiety disorders in the world population.

By now you are thinking that you should not have children. Perish the thought.

LOOK, THE TREATMENT OF BOTH IS A FACT, AND TREATMENTS ARE GETTING BETTER EACH YEAR. A CURE WILL BE FOUND SOME DAY.

The innate abilities of those blessed, yes I said blessed, with the bipolar disorder and mood disorder, and even anxiety disorders, are among the gifted of our times.

I will repeat this message time and time again. It is not just my belief, but proven throughout history.

As you research to educate yourselves, you will be amazed that people the ilk of President Abraham Lincoln, statesmen, playwrights, actors, doctors, musicians, artists, and the giants of civilization in the past and of today are proof that extraordinary potential lies with each of the bipolar and more.

Research, learn and teach your loved ones, and in a while, like a garden, well tended to its best potential, bears fruit. Our relatives, our children, our future lies in education, understanding and treatment, love and support to those needing to grow, and grow they will.

Addictions

Drugs, alcohol, shopping, sex, overeating and others are addictions that may appear in the bipolar disorder. They manifest themselves and we are unable to cope with the results.

Specific understandings of the core issues of our beings, treatment, as well as individual support and medications, 12-step meetings like AA, getting a sponsor, family support and healing environments are the only answers for these problems. The fight back to health must be wanted, and reasons explained for the pressures that drive us literally "to drink".

Life spirals down, the workings of our minds change and the acceptance of certain basic truths as to the why, are often not available until we reach bottom and are willing to listen.

The stresses that push us into addiction are many, and we must learn about the facts, the reasons, the treatments, and remember that we are not alone.

I suggest that you visit sites like the following that address your individual addiction.

There are many facts available, links to other sites and all issues.

This is but a sampling of sites: **www.nmha.org** and look up "Eating Disorders under "fact sheets". A number of addictions are covered on this site.

www.niaaa.gov is a wonderful site for the information on alcoholism. Look up "ALCHOLISM *Getting the Facts",* "FAQ'S on Alcohol Abuse and Alcoholism", "ALCOHOL ALERT," and many other informational articles.

A fine substance abuse web site is at **www.samhsa.gov.** This site offers a lot of information on substance abuse, including "A Substance Abuse Treatment FACILITY LOCATOR," listed by each state.

Addictions and depression costs many millions of dollars to business, and they ruin our lives and tear apart our families. There are a lot of reasons to fight back to life, seek help!

It is said of depression "you have to feel it to heal it." Genetic issues enter the formula as well, but as you reach out and read those web articles, and read the stories of recovery, read the recommended self help books and get treatment, support, and attend those meetings, things start to get better.

I could go on for many pages outlining the pain, damage to families, the legal problems, the lost jobs, the declining health that follows addictions like a wraith to difficult ends, but other sources akin to your needs are better suited for you than I.

You will find your answers as you research, go to meetings, council with your families, heed your doctor, it is not easy, just make the right choice, make that call, and ask for help.

A very sage Doctor offered forth a concept that really makes sense.

Imagine holding an eight-month-old baby, innocent, vulnerable. Would we pour alcohol down it's mouth, would we stick needles into it and fill it with drugs, would we hurt it, would we stuff its mouth with food day after day, would we spend all of the money on shopping or gambling that would take a roof from over the child's head and rob food from it's mouth?

The answer is a rousing, No! Yet that is what we do to ourselves.

There is peace, kindness and healing and recovery out there, lots of it. Seek that help.

Tiles, Toilets, and Fans

The advent of the bipolar condition may be subtle, it may be loud, it might be teary, or a horror until it is explained, medicated and counseled.

The addition of other disorders makes for a mixed bag of concerns.

Visualize a cut deck of cards, in two equal stacks. If you were to shuffle them, they would combine into a random mix. The hand dealt may be as varied as those cards combined and only the knowledge of the game, and practiced fingers make for the knowing. That's what counseling is all about.

Lets look at the cards that can be dealt;

Bipolar disorder, as previously mentioned, is a mood disorder. This means you could be very sad, with tears, (Depression), happy and up or angry or irritated, (Mania) or a mix of them all.

There are a number of mood disorders that may combine with bipolar disorder: personality disorders and anxiety disorders.

By now you should have started to research your concerns, and these other disorders should be looked at and discussed with your mental health professional. Do not fall into the trap that says, "I have a problem and no one knows how I feel." Personality disorders are varied and anxiety disorders the same. There are many of us in the same boat.

I am keeping it simple, but the other disorders are complex.

The best way to inform is by example, and I will get to that in a minute or so.

First, do not despair.

Understand that the human brain has billions of cells all acting in concert. This miracle can be set slightly askew in some areas of the brain with folks like us, and there are medicines that must be used, some times one, two, three, or four at a time during a twenty four hour period.

I can tell you that I have been taking many of the drugs listed for several years, and with time, education and counseling I have been prescribed the best combination of medicines designed to answer my needs. Disorders like schizophrenia may come in later years, they did so with me.

Where do tiles, toilets and fans come in?

I heard voices in a scanning mode, my eyes moving from left to right, up and down and backwards, like reading, but in the mind. Linear surfaces, like looking over the pages of a book, were my information points. I was convinced that I was a super secret agent, a mental giant, with the ability to use telepathy in service to my country. I had many long conversations with world figures; I was filled with largesse, setting business trends, worldwide. I heard messages in the wind, via fans and air conditioners; I received messages from the downward swirling of a toilet, and became a worldwide financier through business trends I received by scanning through the checkerboard pattern of bathroom tiles.

Words, sentences, and advice came to me seemingly to my left and right ears; often I would hear the words whispered to me as in secrecy.

I knew that I was the unstoppable, the untiring sentinel, protector of millions.

You know, it never entered my mind that it all was the fabrication of a hard working brain, needing input to be comfortable.

I never guessed that the thoughts spilling out in facts and figures drew upon the knowledge of my mind; salient facts, bits of trivia, famous names in the news, geography, my education and more.

My mind was a sponge, pulling in information in a way that I never knew could be possible, yet it was proven to be so. When I watched TV, when I read books and newspapers, and when I met folks and more, the information was stored into my mind sometimes with out my knowing where or when the information was garnered, and it arrived in perfect form without my knowledge.

It all seemed real; I had no inkling that it was a natural effect shared by many of us in some way or another.

I had to make a choice, believe my doctors, or to go on living what was so much of a buzz.

I finally became aware that some things were not altogether real.

I was in a spirited conversation, silently, of course, to and fro with a figure of national fame, via telepathy. I was to have a late evening meeting with the person and go out to dine and make decisions about world issues.

At five thirty on a spring evening, I took my place in a chair on the front porch of the health care center that I was being treated at, and settled in to wait for the arrival. I was told that the party would be late.

I received many valid reasons for the tardiness of my contact via telepathy.

Hours passed and still no show, and I dosed, semi awake through the sunset and the rise of a full moon on a blue-black sky, and the North Star winked at me knowingly.

I awoke to a mental message that stated in terse terms that security at the local restaurant had been breached, and that twelve thirty pm was the time for our meeting, at a yet unknown location.

The lights on the porch clicked off. And I sat until I was advised to wait until contacted. I rose, adjusted my suit and tie and walked around the porch to ease the kinks in my legs and back and then settled back into my chair.

I was mentally communicating with security at two o'clock in the morning, again the order was to stand by, and wait for contact.

At two thirty I was sitting bolt upright and attentive, as the meeting occurred in my brain, my face was sweating, my teeth were clenched and I was broadcasting on tight beam to my esteemed contact, who had gone back to a secure site, the dinner was of course cancelled due to affairs of state.

I was giving my input when suddenly I lost my attention. The back of my ankle was being scratched. I signed off and slowly looked down and around to the right ankle. An insistent pulling of my right sock indicated that my legs had not gone dead from sitting, and I tried to focus in the dim light afforded by a nearby streetlight.

I was amazed, it looked like my cat, but I knew that he was asleep back in my room, and this cat seemed a bit stockier.

I slowly bent down to pet the nice black stray kitty. Just as I was about to touch it, I froze; the light had played on the broad white stripe from head to tail of a young skunk. I waited about ten minutes before the fellow got bored from chewing on my sock and waddled away from me. At five thirty am the doors opened, I watched the sunrise and I again regained my life and went inside.

A cosmic truth hit me, nature had done what no one person could do, it threw comedy at me, it chastened me and I started to tell my doctor of my marvels, and fears. A few months later medicines were balanced and the voices started to come under control.

The people, the things, all of the conversations were on a natural plane, they were real; my mind tailored them to me.

My eyes were opened, my life is simpler now, proving the thesis that the disorders don't have to be hell, one must look for the thread of humor that interlaces it all, the threads that entwine to make us who and what we are.

Who to call for help…

Your doctor
Your church
A mental health clinic
Emergency 911
Local hospitals
A psychotherapist
A psychologist
A Mental health hospital
A medical school
A social worker
A police department
A sheriffs department
Call 1-800-Suicide

When Things go Critical

All of us that have grown up with the bipolar disorder, or other disorders or habits, or even the adolescent found in the same circumstances, can be found in a critical stage. At this pivotal time of our lives we must have a place where we can be taken either by loved ones, or as adults we can seek entrance on our own, that will be a place where we can find the answers, listen to others experiences and gain from them, as well as regaining our health, eating habits, regaining or be taught new coping skills, and finding our lost self image.

The many nuances that make up our needs are blind to us, and a place of healing, to awaken and deal with our own special issues is a miracle yet to be understood. We need help and there is a special type of treatment center, a hospital setting that will address all of the above. It is what can be identified as a Critical Care, Fast Response Hospital.

The stay is scheduled for a day to a week, with some on hold until the goals are met.

Feelings of fear, uncertainty, and anguish are felt the first day; this is a natural response to the unknown. Those in the grip of exhaustion are allowed to sleep until they may join in the healing. A medical exam and blood draw is accomplished by the second day and the results are quickly available to your doctor. Your team of talented psychiatrists, a psychologist, a caseworker, mental health nurses, dispensing nurses and other mental health specialists are all ready to help you. Meetings with your case in mind are held each weekday and a psychiatrist visits you every day. The team works like a good Swiss watch in accuracy and feedback on your progress is charted all of every waking day. The patient always has a professional available to them 24/7. You are encouraged to use personal clothes, and the personal quilt or pillow is allowed as well. Laundry service is available.

The work and recovery begins. Scheduled pre-designed classes, support meetings, education and socialization are on line every day, even into the evenings.

You are encouraged to eat healthy, and a galley is available in the dayroom for diabetic snacks, and the required snacks, or liquids and snacks for those in recovery from substance abuse. It is open all day and into the closing hour of the evening.

The whole environment is designed to help the patient back to balance mentally and physically. Excess medications are pared down, and new medications tried until the best course of medication is found for you. A psychologist has a group on weekdays.

If psychological testing is done at your doctors' request, the results are back to him in a short time, ready for his review and action on your behalf.

The days are filled with positives, support, education, personal contact, problem solving and self-assessment.

Goals are stressed, and pre-planning for a life after release is encouraged.

You are informed of the goals of your team and medicines listed each day. Your goals for the day are charted at this time. If you have questions about the medicines that you are taking, or want to know about new ones that have been prescribed for you all you need to do is ask, and a print out about the drug is provided to you. Your doctor reviews the affects of your medicines on you, and decreases or discontinues any that might not been working to the best effect.

Everything is held confidential.

Self-care is promoted. Sleep habits are reviewed every night and the information is ready for your doctor the next morning. In most, the treatment is mentally stimulating, and you are given time to reflect and rest.

A family meeting is scheduled mid way through your stay, or sooner if warranted. The worries, concern and misunderstandings of loved ones and families are answered in this meeting. It is comforting for the patient as well.

Detoxification, as hard as it is, joins the entire program with a special added class each weekday and special cares are provided to help the recovering. An informational class is given to these patients and their needs are expressed, and they learn the reasons why and what powers the addiction. Out patient classes are scheduled for the recovering in all rights.

All during the patients stay, their case manager has been assembling information on them and for them as the going home day approaches. On the last day the patient meets with the case manager and after care is outlined. Doctors and therapists are recommended, appointments made, outside support systems and meetings with the 12-step groups like Alcoholics Anonymous are presented to the recovering and housing verified.

The patient is then released to go back into the environment of loved ones, mentors and the better life now offered as a future.

Some may return, by relapse or misfortune, but healing is there for the great majority.

Note: The model that I have outlined above is in fact a reality.

Mountain Crest
Poudre Valley Hospital
Regional Behavioral Healthcare Center
4601 Corbett Drive
Fort Collins, Colorado 80528

There are doubtless, similar facilities throughout the country.

We're not in Salem any more Toto

The stigma of mental health illness abounds in our society today. It is ingrained in the concepts and thoughts of many people. From news stories, and commentary, to crossword puzzles. Shamefully, there are many insurance companies that still refuse to pay for the treatment of the mentally ill in parity with "normal illnesses." We do not have the ear of the movers and shakers that initiate change. Our politicians, the media, our families, parents and children, must be taught about the truths of mental illness. It is treatable, and should be looked at with understanding, not bias. The prevalent attitude in the work place is damaging. We are afraid to let anyone of our diagnoses be known or that we are in treatment for the healing, it keeps us from that treatment, or in some cases destroys our jobs, ruining our careers. Personnel management, supervisors and owners must be brought up to date of the realities and an understanding of mental illness and its potential for healing and recovery as well.

Although major strides have been made in treatment, and medications, the education and understanding and trust of the population is woefully far behind.

Learned values and concepts in growing up and in life may consider the mentally ill as sick, weak, and uncomfortable to them. We have been considered incompetent, below average, and worse.

Many times families, boyfriends, girlfriends, mate's, fellow workers and the clergy provide support, embracing the patient in treatment and recovery.

At the same time however, varied stigma about the patient in general, or in treatment and recovery may grow into discomfort or mistrust.

A boyfriend, girlfriend husband and wife and our friends may look at reassessing their relationships with us.

We, untreated, get worse, encountering more problems and crisis. Education is the only way to make us aware, seek treatment, or follow doctors and clergy's advice for treatment centers, and hopes for the future. The stresses of the mentally ill coming forth are extreme. The worry of going to a psychiatrist, councilor, a treatment center, or a hospital can be fearful to us or we may be ashamed. We have our soft bias, and the stigma is pressing into that equation as well, but in faith things can really get better.

In a perfect world we would go to a special doctor, get an exam and if advised go to a hospital to get treatment, have our scars, and take a while to live with any disability while healing takes place, and go back to the doctor for checkups. Recovery.

When the normal person goes to a special doctor, gets an exam and if advised goes to a hospital, gets treatments and surgery, has a scar and takes a while to live with any disability while healing takes place and goes back to the doctor for checkups, also recovery.

There should be no stigma or bias involved in each case, because both are essentially the same. Life differs with this and the realities of the things that the public perceives by lack of knowledge and bad input manifest themselves. This process is unconscionable. It should not be so.

Seeking help for a mental disorder and the road to recovery should be seen by mankind as a good and balanced thing to do.

The goal of our population should be to right these wrongs, with support, understanding and acceptance. Our goal is to be treated, and to recover as best we can. These efforts should be unencumbered.

I suggest that Supervisors go to the following web site; The National Institute of Mental Health at **www.nimh.gov** and look under publications for " What to Do When an Employee is Depressed: A Guide for Supervisors."

Supervisors can access the web site **www.Medlineplus.gov** and click on Health you can search in an A to Z format for many pertinent health issues that pertain to their employees issues and needs. Please access the web sites on Stigma listed in the back of the book.

Last thoughts

We are frail, yet we are strong. We know, yet we do not.
We rely on ourselves without any idea that we suffer.
We live our lives sometimes as the lovable Clown, or in pain, or in anger and despair.
We sleep our lives away, or ignore the obvious, being that we know best in all rights.
We suffer the nightmares, misstate our hearts, and lose our families by our actions.
We assess life with the surety of the wise, yet fall short.
We agonize over money, spending it like grains of sand thrown to the wind.
We destroy our careers, yet we feel that the job lost was "Their fault."
We cast anger at our loved ones, big and small, yet we do not understand the pain, concern and fear in their eyes. And the list goes on an on.

How many of you see yourselves in any of the above?
Do expect that for mania we should get a prize?
Do you think that the depressed should get a 10% discount from the Serta or the Beauty Rest Mattress folks?

Do you really want to live any of the above? The answer should be a resounding, No!

You know, perhaps in reading this short book you were touched. Some points educated you, others informed you and by now you are perhaps a little sad or angry with the above.
Let me explain: It is to open your minds to the options available.
When we say, "It is too much for me to do", you are right.
We cannot handle it. When we precede a choice or decision with an " I will", we tend to lie to ourselves, and it never gets done. Start your decisions with " I need."

You see, all of the horrors above will not happen if we ask for help. It is not giving in, it is not a statue of liberty play, it is your life that we are talking about, or a loved ones'.

This whole book is a means to an end; your recovery. You will find that it is a process of self-education, comfort and understanding.
Get in touch with your doctor, just say, " I need your help." If you will go that far, you will find that the forward motion begins. Understanding blossoms within you, and your family.
I wish you good health.
I wish you good healing.
I wish you a full recovery.
And about the money, buy a pen/pencil and a small lined pocket pad. Write down every item, every penny spent and why the purchase was made, and keep track. It is a matter of survival. It awakens us.
Good luck, I know you have it in your heart now. Congratulations, You just made the first step.

Please accept these few words in closing:

Unipolar depression and bipolar 1 and 2 are the most common of mood disorders.

Bipolar 1
Also known as manic-depressive disorder. Bipolar 1 is found when there are many serious episodes per year of mania and/or depression.

Bipolar 2.
Less serious mania, but depression is more common. Fewer episodes per year are evident.

When bipolar mania and depression exist in the same time frame, say a day, it is called a mixed bipolar state.

Rapid cycling of mania and depression many times a year is another form of bipolar disorder state. Ask your doctor about all of these.

Bipolar disorder is very difficult to diagnose because there are other mood disorders with similar symptoms.

Bipolar disorder functions like the pendulum of a clock, moving from mania to depression and back, again and again.

Bipolar disorder can start in childhood yet other target years are 18 to 22.
Adult bipolar disorder can appear at any time, by extreme stress in the workplace, the family or the loss of friends and family or medical trauma, as well as genetic factors.

Family counseling can help the bipolar greatly. This process helps the bipolar person and the family as well.
Try to regulate your day, concentrate, drink decaffeinated coffee and tea, eat regularly, and make every effort to take your medicine on time; do not skip doses of your meds.

If there are people in a family, such as a bipolar grandparent or a parent, Bipolar disorder can appear in the children and their children etc., as genetics are the deciding factor in most cases.

As I mentioned earlier in the book, bipolar disorder can stay with us for a lifetime, occurring again and again. I cannot stress the importance of early diagnosis and treatment. I was not diagnosed until my 50's and it destroyed my life until it was diagnosed and my medicines balanced. Psychotherapy helped immensely.

The symptoms to be aware of as a warning signs for the manic state are: Chronic lack of sleep, nightmares of death or suicide or attempts at suicide, racing thoughts, pressured speech, (fast speech), and over spending money, improper or too many sexual liaisons, using alcohol or drugs and unsound choices in business and life, lack of self image, anger, irritability, and apathy.

The symptoms to be aware of for depression are: sadness, eating too much or too little, exhaustion, lack of energy to deal with the day, withdrawal from society, too much sleep, inability to focus on the day, suicidal thoughts, or attempts.

<u>A word about suicide</u>: Most of the deaths by suicide are found to have been suffering from mood disorders. A preponderance of these deaths result from those

with bipolar disorder. Do not let it happen. Talk to someone, use mental health or suicide hot lines, talk to your doctor or other mental health professional, talk to your family, and do not isolate yourself. Many of these deaths could have been prevented with proper counseling.
The Good Book tells us" there is a time and place for everything" CHOOSE LIFE!

A few words on Schizoaffective Disorder and Schizophrenia.

You are aware of the fact that bipolar disorder is difficult to diagnose.
One of the reasons is that other disorders are similar, yet in some ways different.
Your doctor will work with you to determine your diagnosis, and a proper method of treatment.

Bipolar disorder and schizoaffective disorder are similar, and both can be evident in us at the same time.

Yet, schizophrenia is different. Those of us that do not care what happens in life, cannot speak well when we could before, suffer from living nightmares, seeing and/or hearing voices, do not respond to our loved ones, have trouble thinking things out, and distress our families with aberrant behavior, find life hard. Treatment, the proper medicines and Psychotherapy all combine to help us through each day.

Suggested Reading

Where mankind has triumphed over adversity.

Man's Search for Meaning
And
Man's Search for Ultimate Meaning
By Viktor E. Frankl

Wind Sand and Stars
By Atoine De Saint-Exupery

SOUTH—a memoir of the *Endurance* VOYAGE
By Sir Earnest Shackleton

The Omega-3 Connection
By Andrew Stoll M.D.

Web Sites

To all of the web sites listed,
Thank you all for being there for us. Your help is invaluable.

Note—when you see the indicator.gov at the end of a web address and you find the information that you have been seeking is being found on government web sites. Please understand that the tax dollars that you pay each year are being put to a good use. Other sites ending with.**org, net** or.**com** rely on memberships, donations and grants. They need our donations, just as we need their research and information.

These web sites offer a wealth of information for those that seek the answers on their roads to recovery, and for those that live alongside and support the bipolar. They are but a sampling of the issues that we face, but do not despair. Use those computers and enter the sites that would do you well.

All sites are preceded by http://

www.MedlinePlus.gov This site is a service of the U.S. National Library of Medicine, and the National Institutes of Health. You will find news, health issues a to z, Drugs a to z, a medical encyclopedia, and a medical dictionary. Many links are found on this site. See the Medical encyclopedia and look up omega 3 fatty acids.

www.aafp.org Is the site for the American Academy of Family Physicians.
This site offers information on health issues "From your family doctor".
Type in bipolar, and click. And then click on, "Management of Bipolar Disorder". This article is fifteen pages long, and is well worth the read.

www.familydoctor.org Is the patient information site for the AAFP, Information from your family doctor. See Dysthymic Disorder: When Depression Lingers, many other reports that deal with our issues.

www.world-schzophrenia.org Is the site for the World Fellowship for Schizophrenia and other Allied Disorders. This site contains a symptoms listing for several disorders.

This site is plainly written and lets us know that these issues exist around the world, not just in our country, or in our homes. See "Schizophrenia: First Warning Signs".

www.nmha.org Is the site for The National Mental Health Association.

This site offers wonderful articles and reports on the issues that we face today.

Dial 1-800-969-6642

See the report entitled "Bipolar disorder and Afro Americans", see "Types of treatment", Clinical Depression is a Treatable illness, "Holiday Depression and Stress", "Clinical Depression What you need to know," "Depression, Depression in Women" "Co-Occurrence of Depression with Medical, Psychiatric, and Substance Abuse Disorders," "DO YOU KNOW IT? Frequently Asked Questions About Bipolar Disorder," "Symptoms Learning to Recognize Clinical Depression," " Eating Disorders," and "Schizoaffective Disorders."

www.nimh.nih.gov is the site for the National Institute of Mental Health.

This site offers in depth information on many topics that impact us on a daily basis.

See "What to Do When An Employee is Depressed: A Guide for Supervisors", "Depression", "Going to Extremes Bipolar Disorder", "What to do When a Friend is Depressed: Guide for Students", "Depression: What Every Woman Should Know", "Depression in Men", "It Takes Courage to ask for Help, Real Men, Real Depression", "Stories of Depression", "Let's Talk About Depression", "Treatment of Children with Mental Disorders", "Medications" "Schizophrenia", "WHAT IS IT?" "When Someone Has Schizophrenia", " The Numbers Count"(Mental Disorders in America), "Child-Onset Schizophrenia: An Update from the National Institute of Mental Health," "Brief Notes on the Mental Health of Children and Adolescents." And Many More.

www.nih.gov is the site for the National Institutes of Health, National Institute of Mental Health as above. See NIH News Contact: Jules Asher NIMH Press Office.

See "Gene More Than Doubles Risk pf Depression Following Life Stresses," and look up other news articles about mental health issues.

www.surgeongeneral.gov is the site for The Surgeon General of The United States of America. As in other sites, type in the word bipolar or mood disorders, and you will find a report listed as chapter 4, "Mental Health: A Report of the Surgeon General" Mood Disorders. It is a fine source of information.

www.psych.org is the site for the American Psychiatric Association.
Research it well.

www.helping.apa.org is the site for the American Psychotherapy Association.
See How Therapy Helps (how to find help through Psychotherapy)
This site offers free brochures, and even can help you find a Psychologist.

www.ama-assn.org is the site for the American Medical Association.
Look at the patient information area, and type in your topic.

www.debtorsanonymous.org This is the site for Debtors Anonymous.
Their e-mail is **da-gso@mindspring.com**
Their Phone number is 718-453-2743
Fine brochures, excellent support.

www.aacap.org is the site for the American Academy of Child and Adolescent Psychiatry.
Look for periodicals; one is "The Child" another is "The Adolescent", and see " BIPOLAR DISORDER (MANIC-DEPRESSIVE ILLNESS) in Teens."

www.bpkids.org is the site for the Child and Adolescent Bipolar Foundation. This site offers several important periodicals. Look for "The Storm in my Brain", "Kids and Mood Disorders, Bipolar Disorder and Depression" that is free of charge. It can be downloaded to your computer via pdf file or call for a free copy at 877-927-5437. See "About Early-Onset Bipolar Disorder." This is a good 13 pages, and a very interesting source of information.

www.niaaa.nih.gov is a site dealing with Alcoholism. See "ALCOHOLISM Getting the *Facts*," "FAQ's on Alcohol Abuse and Alcoholism," and under Publications, see " ALCOHOL ALERT".
The periodicals, newsletters and their bookstore make this site a good one to research in. Research Doctor information, use their Mood charts and best of all you can join, but it is free to families.

www.kidshealth.org is the site for Kids Health. This site offers a lot of answers for parents on many disorders and conditions for kids and teens.
See, "Why Am I So Sad", "Bipolar Disorder", and "When Your Child Is Depressed", "Teens Health," "Bipolar Disorder," Teens Health "Coping with an Alcoholic Parent", "Understanding and Preventing Teen Suicide."

www.kidshealth.com See the teen article "Alcohol", and " When your Child is depressed", and lots of reports on kids and teens mental health issues.

www.teenmentalhealth.net Is the site for Teen Mental Health; Parents will find precise information on many topics. See "Signs & Symptoms" of bipolar 1 disorder in teens. "What is Bipolar 1 Disorder", "What is adolescent schizophrenia?" And more.

www.chadd.org is the site for the Children And Adults with Attention-Deficit/ Hyperactivity Disorder.
This site offers fact sheets for members and professionals. Many questions are answered here, and the site is updated regularly.
CHADD 818 Professional Place,
Suite 150 Landover MD
20805
800-233-4050

www.nami.org is the site for "The Nation's Voice on Mental Illness". It is a source of information on mental health, pertinent commentary about adult and the elderly, and this site provides you information on stigma, with a Stigma Busting Network. This network does good work stopping stigma surrounding mental illness in our country. If interested in joining this effort contact-Ms. Stella March at **smarch@nami.org.**

www.dballiance.gov is the site for the Depression and Bipolar Support Alliance. This site offers a screening test for bipolar disorder, and many other reports. There is a great kid's book available. See the report entitled " Finding a Mental Health Professional", a personal guide.

www.aagpgpa.org This is the site of the American Association for Geriatric Psychiatry. You will find many reports, and see "Depression in late life: Not a Natural Part of Aging." This report is for Patients and Caregivers.

www.samhsa.gov. This site is for the Substance Abuse and Mental Health Services Administration, An Agency of the U.S. Department of Human Services. This site offers help for many of those seeking to understand and find answers and tools for Mental Illness and Substance Abuse.
A Substance Abuse Treatment Locator is available, showing sites throughout the United States.

www.mentalhealth.org is the SAMHSA National Mental Health Information Center.
See " Women and Depression Fast Facts," and "Mood Disorders."

www.angelfire.com This site for BPhoenix Advice Columns. See "Stigma". Other topics are discussed.

www.erasethestigma.org Erase the Stigma is an ongoing project of WPSU-FM at Penn State Public Broadcasting. Look up "Resources", and "Did You Know" Best Wishes to WPSU-FM and this site. Their work is invaluable.

www.nida.nih.gov is the site for the National Institute on Drug Abuse. See their newsroom, publications, what's new and see "Understanding Drug Abuse and Addiction."

www.healthyplace.com is a good site to visit. See "A primer on Depression and Bipolar Disorders". " Mood Disorders As Physical Disorders", the stigma of having a mental Illness.

www.mayoclinic.com is the site for the famous Mayo Clinic. Use this site well. They are doing remarkable research on the brain, and understanding how the bipolar disorder relates to it. They offer reports on many of our issues. See "Exercise eases symptoms of anxiety and depression", and "Depression in kids: How is it treated."

www.web.sfn.org is the site for the Society for Neuroscience. This site deals with information on the Brain and the nervous system.

www.X-Plain.com is the site for The Patient Education Institute Inc. See "*Depression* Reference summary". (Depression)

www.mentalhealth.com This is the site INTERNET MENTAL HEALTH.
Best wishes to the founder of this site and other sites, a teacher, and a textbook

author, an internationally known healer to the mentally ill, and the recipient of many awards, Phillip W. Long M.D. See his report " MAJOR DEPRESSIVE DISORDER Diagnostic Questions", and many of his reports and articles. Look up the links on this site.

www.fda.gov is the site for the U.S. Food and Drug Administration. See their consumer magazines such as "The Lowdown on Depression" By Carol Lewis.

0-595-30649-7

www.ingramcontent.com/pod-product-compliance
Lightning Source LLC
Chambersburg PA
CBHW021230280526
45784CB00005B/2032

* 9 7 8 0 5 9 5 3 0 6 4 9 7 *